BERABERA BOOK-2.5
ベラベラブック-2.5

BERABERA BOOK-2.5
contents
モクジ

P4 **BERABERA more PHRASES-1**

P22 **SHORT-CUT to BERABERA** [take]

P26 **BERABERA one point check-1**
Conjugating irregular verbs

P28 **BERABERA more PHRASES-2**

P44 **SHORT-CUT to BERABERA** [make]

P48 **BERABERA one point check-2**
Adjectives and their opposites

P50 **BERABERA more PHRASES-3**

P68 **SHORT-CUT to BERABERA** [get]

P72 **BERABERA one point check-3**
Here are 8 important prepositions

P74 **BERABERA more PHRASES-4**

P90 *BERABERA one point check-4*
Homonyms

P91 *SHORT-CUT to BERABERA [have]*

P94 *BERABERA one point check-5*
Various adverbs

P96 BERABERA more PHRASES-5

P114 *BERABERA one point check-6*
Everyday expressions

P116 BERABERA more PHRASES-6

P134 BERABERA TRAVEL

P138 *The list of KATAKANA*

P140 MEZASE! TRILINGUAL!!

P142 EIGO DE UTAOU!

● *At the end of this book (p.138-139), there is the list of KATAKANA (square Japanese syllabary). Use it to perfect your KATAKANA pronunciation.*

ベラベラmoreフレーズ-1
BERABERA more PHRASES -1

**Now that you've studied English for a while,
How did you feel in New York?**

*Even though it's an English-speaking place
I felt pretty relaxed while being in New York.
I didn't feel before, but this time was different.
Drinking after work, banter like,
"Having a good time? Oh yeah."
Seemed to flow easily and naturally.
The next day, everyone said I'd talked a lot the night before
but I couldn't really remember what I said.
But I did remember the feeling,
"Hey, I'm speaking English!"*

What you say to everyone when you finally finish work:

Good job!

What you say to the waiter when he comes for your order:

I'll start with a draft beer.

What you say when someone makes a great play:

Awesome!

What you say after looking at your watch:

I gotta go!

オツカレサマ。
O-TSU-KA-RE-SA-MA

This is a set phrase.

トリアエズ ナマビール。
TO-RI-A-E-ZU NA-MA-BI-I-RU

"A draft beer"=ナマビール。

スゲェ!
SU-GE-E

This phrase is usually used by young men.

イカナクチャ!
I-KA-NA-KU-CHA

"Go"=イク。

What you say when you're tired of walking:

Let's take a taxi.

What you say when you have a little accident:

Oops!

What you say to your friend when he looks blue:

Don't let it get you down.

What you say when you really screwed up:

I wasn't thinking.

タクシーデ イコウ。
TA-KU-SHI-I-DE I-KO-U

"A taxi"=タクシー。

オット！
O-tTO

「ウワァ！(U-WA-A)」「キャー！(KYA-A)」etc.

クヨクヨ スルナヨ。
KU-YO-KU-YO SU-RU-NA-YO

"Look blue"=クヨクヨスル。

ウッカリ シテタヨ。
U-kKA-RI SHI-TE-TA-YO

"Be not thinking"=ウッカリ。

What you say when you just barely made it:

That was close.

What you say when you keep getting told the same thing:

Not again!

What you say to your friend as you indicate the pen he borrowed:

Give it back.

What you say after beating a close rival:

Here's to today's win!

キキイッパツ ダッタ。
KI-KI-I-pPA-TSU DA-tTA

キキ="a crisis"。

マタカヨ!
MA-TA-KA-YO

"Again"=マタ。This is a set phrase for young men.

ソレ カエシテ。
SO-RE KA-E-SHI-TE

"Give back"=カエス。

キョウノ ショウリニ カンパイ!
KYO-U-NO SHO-U-RI-NI KA-N-PA-I

カンパイ="a toast"。"Today"=キョウ。

What you say when the person you called isn't there:

May I leave a message?

What you say about a fantastic view:

I can't find the words.

What you say to a friend who isn't paying attention:

Watch out!

What you say when asked, "Where are you from?":

Guess where?

デンゴンヲ ノコセマスカ？
DE-N-GO-N-WO NO-KO-SE-MA-SU-KA

"A message"＝デンゴン。

コトバニ デキナイヨ…。
KO-TO-BA-NI DE-KI-NA-I-YO

"Words"＝コトバ。

アブナイ！
A-BU-NA-I

「キヲツケテ！(KI-WO-TSU-KE-TE)」「チュウイシテ！(CHU-U-I-SHI-TE)」etc.

ドコダト オモウ？
DO-KO-DA-TO O-MO-U

「ナンダト オモウ？」="Guess what?"、「ダレダト オモウ？」="Guess who?"。

What you say when you see a fire:

Let's get out of here!

What you say when you arrive in New York:

Hey, I'm in NY!

What you say to someone who won't stop chasing after you:

Stop following me!

What you say when someone is talking pointlessly:

So what?

ニゲロ！
NI-GE-RO

ニゲル="run away"。

ニューヨークニ ツイタゾッ！
NYU-U-YO-O-KU-NI TSU-I-TA-ZO†

"Arrive"＝ツク。

ツイテ コナイデ！
TSU-I-TE KO-NA-I-DE

"Follow"＝ツイテクル。

ダカラ ナンナノ？
DA-KA-RA NA-N-NA-NO

"So"＝ダカラ。

What you say after you order but notice you don't have much time:

Can I have it right away?

What you say at the ticket counter:

How much is a round trip ticket?

What you say when you go somewhere for the first time:

Is there a taxi stand around here?

What you say at the hotel front desk:

I'd like to stay one more night.

スグ デキマスカ?
SU-GU DE-KI-MA-SU-KA

"Right away"=スグ。

オウフクキップハ イクラデスカ?
O-U-FU-KU-KI-pPU-WA I-KU-RA-DE-SU-KA

"A round trip"=オウフク。"A ticket"=キップ。

コノヘンニ タクシーノリバハ アリマスカ?
KO-NO-HE-N-NI TA-KU-SHI-I-NO-RI-BA-WA A-RI-MA-SU-KA

"A taxi stand"=タクシーノリバ。

モウイチニチ トマリタインデスケド。
MO-U-I-CHI-NI-CHI TO-MA-RI-TA-I-N-DE-SU-KE-DO

"More"=モウ。"One night"=イッパク。

What you say when calling a popular restaurant:

Can I make a reservation?

What you say when it seems like you're never going to get to your destination:

How long until we arrive?

What you say when you go to a restaurant late at night:

What time do you close?

What you say when you screw up at work:

I apologize.

ヨヤクハ デキマスカ？
YO-YA-KU-WA DE-KI-MA-SU-KA

"A reservation"=ヨヤク。

アト ドレクライデ ツキマスカ？
A-TO DO-RE-KU-RA-I-DE TSU-KI-MA-SU-KA

"How long"=ドレクライ。

ナンジニ ヘイテンデスカ？
NA-N-JI-NI HE-I-TE-N-DE-SU-KA

"What time"=ナンジ。

モウシワケナイ。
MO-U-SHI-WA-KE-NA-I

This is a Japanese traditional set phrase.

What you say when someone makes a remarkable improvement in his English:

Keep it up!

What you say when someone asks, "Can I stay at your house tonight?":

Be my guest.

What you say when you hear that the president of your company was saying good things about you:

You make my day.

What you say when the train doors close just before you can get on:

God damn it!

ソノチョウシ！
SO-NO-CHO-U-SHI

「イイカンジ！(I-I-KA-N-JI)」「ガンバレ！(GA-N-BA-RE)」etc.

ドウゾ、ドウゾ。
DO-U-ZO DO-U-ZO

「イイデスヨ (I-I-DE-SU-YO)」「ヨロコンデ (YO-RO-KO-N-DE)」etc.

ウレシイナア！
U-RE-SHI-I-NA-A

「ヤッタ！(YA-tTA)」「シアワセ！(SHI-A-WA-SE)」etc.

チクショー！
CHI-KU-SHO-U

This phrase is spoken to oneself.

ショートカット トゥ ベラベラ
SHORT-CUT to BERABERA

take
[teik]

the past tense took [tuk]
the past participle taken [teikən]
the present participle taking [teikiŋ]

verb =「**モッテイク**」「**トル**」
　　　　MO-tTE-I-KU　TO-RU

~ヲ モッテイク **~WO MOtTEIKU**	**ボクハ シゴトニ カバンヲ モッテイク.** **BOKUWA SHIGOTONI KABANWO MOtTEIKU** I take my bag to work.
~ヲ ツレテイク **~WO TSURETEIKU**	**カノジョハ アカンボウヲ ツレテイク.** **KANOJOWA AKANBOUWO TSURETEIKU** She takes her baby.
~ヲ トル **~WO TORU**	**ボクハ イットウショウヲ トリマシタ.** **BOKUWA ItTOUSHOUWO TORIMASHITA** I took the first prize.
~ヲ カウ **~WO KAU**	**ワタシタチハ イエヲ カッタ.** **WATASHITACHIWA IEWO KAtTA** We took the house.
~ヲ カリル **~WO KARIRU**	**アパートヲ カリマス.** **APAATOWO KARIMASU** I'll take the apartment.
~ヲ ノム **~WO NOMU**	**クスリヲ ノミナサイ.** **KUSURIWO NOMINASAI** Take some medicine.
~ヲ ヒツヨウトスル **~WO HITSUYOUTOSURU**	**ナガイジカンヲ ヒツヨウトスル.** **NAGAIJIKANWO HITSUYOUTOSURU** It takes a long time.
~ヲ サイヨウスル **~WO SAIYOUSURU**	**カレノ サイヨウヲ キメタ.** **KARENO SAIYOUWO KIMETA** We've decided to take him.
~ニ ノル **~NI NORU**	**ワタシハ バスニ ノリマス.** **WATASHiWA BASUNI NORIMASU** I take a bus.
~ニ スワル **~NI SUWARU**	**ドウゾ オスワリ クダサイ.** **DOUZO OSUWARI KUDASAI** Take a seat, please.

"Take" has many meanings in English.
Once you remember these meanings
you'll be one step closer to speaking like a native.

TAKE BERABERA

take B to A	Aノトコロニ Bヲ モッテイク. A-NOTOKORONI B-WO MOtTEIKU	
take A for B	Aヲ Bト リカイスル. A-WO B-TO RIKAISURU	
take A from B	Bカラ Aヲ ヘラス. B-KARA A-WO HERASU	
take off	ヌグ. NUGU	
take in	トリイレル. キュウシュウスル. TORIIRERU, KYUUSHUUSURU	
take out	トリダス. ツレダス. TORIDASU, TSUREDASU	
take down	オロス. OROSU	
take over	ハコンデツレテイク. ヒキツグ. HAKONDETSURETEIKU, HIKITSUGU	
take to	スキニナル. SUKININARU	
take up	ヒロイアゲル. HIROIAGERU	
take a rest	ヤスム. YASUMU	
take a shower	シャワーヲ アビル. SHAWAAWO ABIRU	
take a walk	サンポヲ スル. SANPOWO SURU	
take away	ショクタクヲ カタヅケル. SHOKUTAKUWO KATADUKERU	
take after	(オヤニ) ニル. (OYANI) NIRU	
take back	トリケス. モドス. TORIKESU, MODOSU	
take care of	メンドウヲ ミル. MENDOUWO MIRU	

ショートカットトゥペラペラ
SHORT-CUT to BERABERA

What you say when nothing seems to go right:

I wanna take a day off.

What you say when asked, "Where is the station?":

This road takes you to the station.

What you say to your friend as he's about to make his appearance on the show:

Take a deep breath.

What you say to your guest:

What do you take in your coffee?

take

イチニチ ヤスミガ ホシイヨ。
I-CHI-NI-CHI YA-SU-MI-GA HO-SHI-I-YO

"A day off"=ヤスミ。

コノミチヲ イケバ ツキマス。
KO-NO-MI-CHI-WO I-KE-BA TSU-KI-MA-SU

"This"=コノ。"A road"=ミチ。

シンコキュウ シテ!
SHI-N-KO-KYU-U SHI-TE

"A breath"=コキュウ、"breathe"=コキュウスル。

コーヒーニ ナニカ イレル?
KO-O-HI-I-NI NA-NI-KA I-RE-RU

"Take in"=イレル。

ベラベラワンポイントチェック-1
BERABERA one point check-1 [Conjugating irregular verbs]

do　スル SURU → シタ SHITA
キノウ ソノシゴトヲ シタ. (KINOU SONOSHIGOTOWO SHITA)
I did that work yesterday.

think　カンガエル KANGAERU → カンガエタ KANGAETA
ワタシハ ソウ カンガエタ. (WATASHIWA SOU KANGAETA)
I thought so.

keep　トッテオク TOtTEOKU → トッテオイタ TOtTEOITA
ソレヲ アトニ トッテオイタ. (SOREWO ATONI TOtTEOITA)
I kept it for later.

give　クレル KURERU → クレタ KURETA
カノジョハ ホンヲ クレタ. (KANOJOWA HONWO KURETA)
She gave me a book.

cut　キル KIRU → キッタ KItTA
ワタシワ ユビヲ キッタ. (WATASHIWA YUBIWO KItTA)
I cut my finger.

write　カク KAKU → カイタ KAITA
カレハ ショウセツヲ カイタ. (KAREWA SHOUSETSUWO KAITA)
He wrote a novel.

wear　キル KIRU → キタ KITA
カレハ コートヲ キタ. (KAREWA KOOTOWO KITA)
He wore a coat.

tell　イウ IU → イッタ ItTA
ダカラ イッタデショ. (DAKARA ItTADESHO)
I told you so.

Japanese has some rules for conjugating verbs.
Here are some examples.

hold　ツカム (TSUKAMU) → ツカンダ (TSUKANDA)

カノジョハ テヲ ツカンダ. (KANOJOWA TEWO TSUKANDA)
She **held** my hand.

run　ハシル (HASHIRU) → ハシッタ (HASHItTA)

カレヲ タスケルタメニ ハシッタ. (KAREWO TASUKERUTAMENI HASHItTA)
I **ran** to rescue him.

find　ミツケル (MITSUKERU) → ミツケタ (MITSUKETA)

ボクハ サイフヲ ミツケタ. (BOKUWA SAIFUWO MITSUKETA)
I **found** my wallet.

know　シル (SHIRU) → シッタ (SHItTA)

ソレヲ スデニ シッテイタ. (SOREWO SUDENI SHItTEITA)
I **knew** that already.

carry　オクル (OKURU) → オクッタ (OKUtTA)

カノジョヲ イエニ オクッタ. (KANOJOWO IENI OKUtTA)
I **carried** my girlfriend home.

speak　ハナス (HANASU) → ハナシタ (HANASHITA)

スデニ カレニ ハナシタ. (SUDENI KARENI HANASHITA)
I **spoke** to him already.

lose　ウシナウ (USHINAU) → ウシナッタ (USHINAtTA)

カレハ バランスヲ ウシナッタ. (KAREWA BARANSUWO USHINAtTA)
He **lost** his balance.

win　カツ (KATSU) → カッタ (KAtTA)

カレガ マタ カッタ. (KAREGA MATA KAtTA)
He **won** again.

ベラベラmoreフレーズ-2
BERABERA more PHRASES-2
So, after 2 years of study, how would you rate your English ability?

About hearing...
Truthfully, I can really only make out about half of the
"SmaSTATION-2" hearing questions,
but lately my confidence is growing little by little.
And compared to before, I'm totally getting 'em!
Phrases just pop into my head.
Everyone knows I've been studying flash cards
but I didn't really understand the meaning.
That's why I often can't answer the questions in Japanese.
It's hard to explain. Everyone says my hearing is really good
but I still don't give myself more than a score of 2.
If I evaluate myself badly, I can keep pushing myself harder...

What you say as you hand someone a present:

This is for you.

What you say at a wedding when suddenly asked to give a speech:

I'm too shy.

What you say when inexplicable coincidences happen one after another:

It's destiny!

What you say when you see your friend:

How's it going?

コレヲ アナタニ。
KO-RE-WO A-NA-TA-NI

"For〜"=〜ノタメニ、"for you"=アナタノ タメニ。

ハズカシー。
HA-ZU-KA-SHI-I

In this case, you shold almost scream it.

ウンメイヲ カンジル!
U-N-ME-I-WO KA-N-JI-RU

"Destiny"=ウンメイ。

チョウシ ドウ?
CHO-U-SHI DO-U

「ゲンキ？(GE-N-KI)」「ドウシテタ？(DO-U-SHI-TE-TA)」etc.

What you say when you want to know if Chonan Kang is around:

Have you seen Chonan?

What you say when the club you're at is dead:

Let's go somewhere else.

What you say when you hear really bad news:

That's terrible.

What you say when your friend tells you he'll be fluent in 6 months:

Don't make me laugh!

チョナンニ アッタ？
CHO-NA-N-NI A-tTA

"See"=アウ (in this case)。

ホカノ ミセニ イコウ。
HO-KA-NO MI-SE-NI I-KO-U

"Else"=ホカノ。

コリャ、ヒドイ。
KO-RYA HI-DO-I

コリャ="this is" or "that's"。

ワラワセルナヨ！
WA-RA-WA-SE-RU-NA-YO

"Laugh"=ワラウ、"make～laugh"=ワラワセル。

What you say when you come back to your car and find it all scratched up:

That really makes me angry.

What you say when your sunburnt back starts getting better and itchy:

My back *is* itchy!

What you say when you hear good news:

Sweet!

What you say to someone telling you why he's late:

No more excuses!

アタマニ キタ!
A-TA-MA-NI KI-TA

「オコッタ！(O-KO-tTA)」「ムカツク！(MU-KA-TSU-KU)」etc.

セナカガ カユイ!
SE-NA-KA-GA KA-YU-I

"A back"＝セナカ。

イイネ!
I-I-NE

「カッコイイ！(KA-kKO-I-I)」「ステキ！(SU-TE-KI)」etc.

イイワケ スルナ!
I-I-WA-KE SU-RU-NA

"An excuse"＝イイワケ。

What you say after a lengthy explanation:

Something like that.

What you say when you can't wait to dig into the feast in front of you:

Looks great!

What you say at the end of an argument:

Let's make up.

What you say the first time you get a massage:

That tickles!

ダイタイ ソンナモン。
DA-I-TA-I SO-N-NA-MO-N

「ッテコトデ (tTE-KO-TO-DE)」「ソンナカンジカナ (SO-N-NA-KA-N-JI-KA-NA)」etc.

オイシソウ!
O-I-SHI-SO-U

オイシイ="delicious"。

ナカナオリ シヨウ。
NA-KA-NA-O-RI SHI-YO-U

"Let's～."=～シヨウ。

クスグッタアイ!
KU-SU-GU-tTA-A-I

"Tickle"=クスグル。

What you say in your waiting room when you're looking for Mr. Nakai:

Is Mr. Nakai around?

What you say to the guy next to you while watching a soccer game:

Who's your favorite player?

What you say when you find something interesting at a flea market:

Can I pick it up?

What you say to the pharmacist:

Do you have any cold medicine?

ナカイクン イル？
NA-KA-I-KU-N I-RU

"Mr.〜"=〜クン (for young men)。

スキナ センシュハ ダレ？
SU-KI-NA SE-N-SHU-WA DA-RE

"Who"=ダレ。

テニ トッテモ イイデスカ？
TE-NI TO-tTE-MO I-I-DE-SU-KA

"Pick〜up"=テニ トル。

カゼグスリ アリマスカ？
KA-ZE-GU-SU-RI A-RI-MA-SU-KA

"Medicine"=クスリ、"cold medicine"=カゼグスリ。

What you say to the hotel front desk when your stomach hurts:

I need a doctor.

What you yell when you find someone fallen in the street:

Call an ambulance!

What you say when you lose your passport while traveling abroad:

Where is the Japanese Embassy?

Suddenly it starts raining. What you say when someone offers, "Hey, share my umbrella?":

That'd be great.

**オイシャサンヲ
オネガイシマス。**
O-I-SHA-SA-N-WO O-NE-GA-I-SHI-MA-SU

"A doctor"=オイシャサン。

キュウキュウシャ ヨンデ!
KYU-U-KYU-U-SHA YO-N-DE

"An ambulance"=キュウキュウシャ。

**ニッポンタイシカンハ
ドコデスカ?**
NI-pPO-N-TA-I-SHI-KA-N-WA DO-KO-DE-SU-KA

"An embassy"=タイシカン。

ソレハ アリガタイ。
SO-RE-WA A-RI-GA-TA-I

"That"=ソレ。

What you say when your friend succeeds in losing 10 kilograms:

You did it!

What you say when a hamburger isn't enough:

I'll take some french fries, too.

What you say when asked your opinion of the movie:

That movie was a real disappointment.

What you say when you really wanna know what became of the girl your friend met at a party:

What happened with that girl?

ヤッタネ!
YA-tTA-NE

「スゴイネ!(SU-GO-I-NE)」「スバラシイ!(SU-BA-RA-SHI-I)」etc.

ポテトモ クダサイ。
PO-TE-TO-MO KU-DA-SA-I

"French fries"=(フライド) ポテト。

アノエイガハ キタイハズレ デシタ。
A-NO-E-I-GA-WA KI-TA-I-HA-ZU-RE DE-SHI-TA

"That"=アノ。"A movie"=エイガ。

アノコト ドウナッテルノ?
A-NO-KO-TO DO-U-NA-tTE-RU-NO

"That girl"=アノコ。

SHORT-CUT to BERABERA

make
[meik]

the past tense made [meid]
the past participle made [meid]
the present participle making [meikiŋ]
verb =
[ツクル]　[トウタツスル]　[オコナウ]
TSU-KU-RU　TO-U-TA-TSU-SU-RU　O-KO-NA-U

~ヲ ツクル ~WO TSUKURU	ボクハ パンヲ ツクリマス. BOKUWA PANWO TSUKURIMASU **I make bread.**
~ヲ モウケル ~WO MOUKERU	カレハ タクサン モウケタ. KAREWA TAKUSAN MOUKETA **He made a lot of money.**
~ヲ オコス ~WO OKOSU	キミハ イツモ トラブルヲ オコス. KIMIWA ITSUMO TORABURUWO OKOSU **You always make trouble.**
~ヲ トトノエル ~WO TOTONOERU	ベッドヲ トトノエナサイ. BEdDOWO TOTONOENASAI **Make your bed.**
~ニ マニアウ ~NI MANIAU	サイシュウデンシャニ マニアッタ. SAISHUUDENSHANI MANIaITA **I made the last train.**
~ヲ セイコウサセル ~WO SEIKOUSASERU	ソレガ ショウヲ セイコウサセル. SOREGA SHOUWO SEIKOUSASERU **It makes the show.**
~ノ オトヲ タテル ~NO OTOWO TATERU	シズカニ シテ. SHIZUKANI SHITE **Stop making that noise.**
~ナ キブンニ サセル ~NA KIBUNNI SASERU	キミハ イライラサセル. KIMIWA IRAIRASASERU **You make me nervous.**

> "Make" also has many meanings in English besides just "tsukuru". Your Japanese won't be perfect without all of them.

make BERABERA

make B for A	Aニ Bヲ ツクッテアゲル。(ヨウイシテアゲル) A-NI B-WO TSUKUtTEAGERU (YOUISHITEAGERU)
make for A	Aノホウヘ ススンデイク。 A-NOHOUE SUSUNDEIKU
make A from B	Bヲ ゲンリョウニ Aヲ ツクル。 B-WO GENRYOUNI A-WO TSUKURU
make A of B	Bヲ ザイリョウニ Aヲ ツクル。 B-WO ZAIRYOUNI A-WO TSUKURU
make A into B	Aヲ Bニ スル。 A-WO B-NI SURU
make a promise	ヤクソクスル。 YAKUSOKUSURU
make a mistake	シッパイスル。 SHIpPAISURU
make a phone call	デンワスル。 DENWASURU
make a reservation	ヨヤクスル。 YOYAKUSURU
make a videotape	ロクガスル。 ROKUGASURU
make a wish	ネガイゴトヲ スル。 NEGAIGOTOWO SURU
make a line	レツニ ナラブ。 RETSUNI NARABU
make a request	ヨウキュウスル。 YOUKYUUSURU
make fun of	カラカウ。 KARAKAU
make up	ナカナオリスル。 NAKANAORISURU
make out	リカイスル。 RIKAISURU
make sure of	タシカメル。 TASHIKAMERU

ショートカットトゥベラベラ
SHORT-CUT to BERABERA

Your friend helps you move. What you say when you return the favor:

This makes us even.

What you say when you're gonna be late...but maybe...:

Can we make it?

What you say when trusting an important assignment to a co-worker:

Don't make a mistake.

What you say when children ask, "What's cheese made from?":

Cheese is made from milk.

make

コレデ チャラダネ。
KO-RE-DE CHA-RA-DA-NE

"Even"＝チャラ。

マダ マニアイマス？
MA-DA MA-NI-A-I-MA-SU

"Make"＝マニアウ。

マチガエナイデ！
MA-CHI-GA-E-NA-I-DE

"Make a mistake"＝マチガエル。

チーズハ ギュウニュウカラ ダヨ！
CHI-I-ZU-WA GYU-U-NYU-U-KA-RA DA-YO

"Milk"＝ギュウニュウ。

べラべラワンポイントチェック-2
BERABERA one point check-2 [Adjectives and their opposites]

easy ヤサシイ YASASHII	↔	difficult ムズカシイ MUZUKASHII
light カルイ KARUI	↔	heavy オモイ OMOI
hard カタイ KATAI	↔	soft ヤワラカイ YAWARAKAI
glad ウレシイ URESHII	↔	sad カナシイ KANASHII
sharp スルドイ SURUDOI	↔	dull ニブイ NIBUI
full イッパイノ IpPAINO	↔	empty カラノ KARANO
noisy ウルサイ URUSAI	↔	quiet シズカナ SHIZUKANA
interesting オモシロイ OMOSHIROI	↔	boring タイクツナ TAIKUTSUNA
early ハヤイ HAYAI	↔	late オソイ OSOI
deep フカイ FUKAI	↔	shallow アサイ ASAI

How many common adjectives can you understand?
Let's check their antonyms at the same time.

warm アタタカイ ATATAKAI	↔	**cool** スズシイ SUZUSHII
dry カワイタ KAWAITA	↔	**wet** ヌレタ NURETA
possible カノウナ KANOUNA	↔	**impossible** フカノウナ FUKANOUNA
private コジンテキナ KOJINTEKINA	↔	**public** コウキョウノ KOUKYOUNO
cheap ヤスイ YASUI	↔	**expensive** タカイ TAKAI
clean キレイ KIREI	↔	**dirty** キタナイ KITANAI
true ホントウノ HONTOUNO	↔	**false** ニセノ NISENO
thick アツイ ATSUI	↔	**thin** ウスイ USUI
wide ヒロイ HIROI	↔	**narrow** セマイ SEMAI
distant トオイ TOOI	↔	**near** チカイ CHIKAI

ベラベラmoreフレーズ-3
BERABERA more PHRASES -3
How has your study method changed since you started with the flash cards?

I started with grammar
but I hated it so much that the only way to
make any progress was to use the flash cards.
They were good for me.
Now I'm studying grammar again, and
when I look at phrases that I had simply memorized, I keep realizing,
"Oh, that's why it's that way!"
As I understand more and more it's becoming interesting again.
So even when I get really busy with work,
the urge to study lately is almost overwhelming!
It's an important milestone for me.

What you say when you're taking a taxi and the traffic is just too much:

Where is the nearest subway station?

What you say at immigration when asked how long your stay will be:

I plan to stay for a week.

What you say when you run into Mr. Nakai at a restaurant:

Would you join us?

What you say when you can't quite make out what your friend is trying to say:

I don't get you.

イチバン チカイ チカテツノ エキハ ドコデスカ?
I-CHI-BA-N CHI-KA-I CHI-KA-TE-TSU-NO E-KI-WA DO-KO-DE-SU-KA

"The nearest"=イチバン チカイ。"A subway"=チカテツ。

イッシュウカンノ ヨテイデス。
I-sSHU-U-KA-N-NO YO-TE-I-DE-SU

"A week"=イッシュウカン。

イッショニ ドウ?
I-sSHO-NI DO-U

"Join～"=イッショニ～スル。

イッテルコトガ ワカラナイヨ!
I-tTE-RU-KO-TO-GA WA-KA-RA-NA-I-YO

"Get"=リカイスル（ワカル）。

What you say when suddenly you can't hear anything:

My earphones don't work.

What you say at the souvenir shop when traveling abroad:

Can I use yen here?

What you say to the exceptionally kind taxi driver:

Keep the change, please.

What you say after eating everything on the table:

I'm full.

イヤホンガ コワレテイマス。
I-YA-HO-N-GA KO-WA-RE-TE-I-MA-SU

"Earphones"=イヤホン。

エンハ ツカエマスカ?
E-N-WA TSU-KA-E-MA-SU-KA

"Use"=ツカウ。

オツリハ トットイテ。
O-TSU-RI-WA TO-tTO-I-TE

"Change"=オツリ。

オナカ イッパイ。
O-NA-KA I-pPA-I

"Full"=イッパイ。

55

What you say to your friend who is brimming over with confidence:

Wanna make a bet?

What you say to your friend who's making fun of you:

Are you teasing me?

What you say when you get all the answers right:

Are you impressed?

What you say when you're so taken with something, and trembling:

I was moved!

カケル？
KA-KE-RU

カネヲ カケル="play for money".

カラカッテンノ？
KA-RA-KA-tTE-N-NO

「フザケテルノ？ (FU-ZA-KE-TE-RU-NO)」「ホンキナノ？ (HO-N-KI-NA-NO)」etc.

カンシン シタ？
KA-N-SHI-N SHI-TA

"Impress"=カンシン サセル。

カンドウ シタ！
KA-N-DO-U SHI-TA

"Be moved"=カンドウ スル。

What you say when the flight you want to get on is already fully booked:

Could you put me on the waiting list?

What you say when you won't be able to see a friend for a while:

Give me a hug.

What you say at a restaurant as you're looking over the menu:

Is there anything you don't like?

What you say to the police when your wallet has been pickpocketed:

It's an emergency!

キャンセルマチヲ シタイノデスガ。
KYA-N-SE-RU-MA-CHI-WO SHI-TA-I-NO-DE-SU-GA

"On the waiting list"＝キャンセルマチ。

ギュッテ シテ。
GYU-tTE SHI-TE

This phrase is usually used by young women.

キライナモノ アル？
KI-RA-I-NA-MO-NO A-RU

"Not like"＝キライ。

キンキュウ デス！
KI-N-KYU-U DE-SU

"Be pickpocketed"＝スラレル。

What you say when it's too hot in the taxi:

Could you turn on the air conditioner?

What you say to the girl next to you whose perfume you can't get enough of:

What perfume are you wearing?

What you say when riding in a taxi and you see a store that looks interesting:

Could you let me off here?

What you say when you find an interesting homepage:

Have you seen the "Sma STAY" website already?

エアコンヲ イレテ クダサイ。
E-A-KO-N-WO I-RE-TE KU-DA-SA-I

"An air conditioner"=エアコン。

コウスイハ ナニヲ ツカッテルノ?
KO-U-SU-I-WA NA-NI-WO TSU-KA-tTE-RU-NO

"Perfume"=コウスイ。

ココデ オロシテ モラエマスカ?
KO-KO-DE O-RO-SHI-TE MO-RA-E-MA-SU-KA

"Off"=オリル、"let〜off"=オロス。

スマステノ ホームページ ミタコト アル?
SU-MA-SU-TE-NO HO-O-MU-PE-E-JI MI-TA-KO-TO A-RU

"A website"=ホームページ。

What you say when you need to end a party:

The party's over.

What you say when asked how yesterday's party was:

It was boring.

What you say at a restaurant when you can't finish your food:

Can I take this home?

What you say to your friend when he picks up the tab:

I'll treat next time.

ソロソロ オヒラキニ シマス。
SO-RO-SO-RO O-HI-RA-KI-NI SHI-MA-SU

"End a party" = オヒラキ。

ツマンナカッタ。
TSU-MA-N-NA-KA-tTA

"Boring" = ツマラナイ。

コレヲ モチカエッテモ イイデスカ?
KO-RE-WO MO-CHI-KA-E-tTE-MO I-I-DE-SU-KA

"Take ~home" = モチカエル。

コンドハ ゴチソウ スルネ。
KO-N-DO-WA GO-CHI-SO-U SU-RU-NE

"Next time" = コンド。

What you say when you get to the hotel you've reserved a room at:

I have a reservation for tonight.

What you say when on a scale of 1 to 10, you're 10 happy:

I've never been this happy!

What you say when someone tells a bad joke:

That was bad.

What you say when your friend arrives at just the appointed time:

Right on time.

コンヤ ヨヤク シテアリマス。
KO-N-YA YO-YA-KU SHI-TE-A-RI-MA-SU

"Tonight"＝コンヤ。

サイコウノ キブンダ！
SA-I-KO-U-NO KI-BU-N-DA

サイコウ＝"highest","supreme","maximum" etc.

サム〜イ。
SA-MU-U-I

This phrase is used by boys and girls.

ジカン ドオリ ダネ。
JI-KA-N DO-U-RI DA-NE

This is a set phrase. "Time"＝ジカン。

What you say when deciding when and where to meet:

How about Shibuya at 6 o'clock?

What you say when you want someone to guess the distance:

How far is it to Shinjuku?

What you say after deciding to walk to your destination:

How long a walk is it from here?

What you say when asking for directions:

Will you draw a map?

ロクジニ シブヤデ イイ？
RO-KU-JI-NI SHI-BU-YA-DE I-I

"6 o'clock"＝ロク ジ。

シンジュクマデ ドレクライ？
SHI-N-JU-KU-MA-DE DO-RE-KU-RA-I

"How far"＝ドレクライ。

ココカラ アルイテ ドレクライ？
KO-KO-KA-RA A-RU-I-TE DO-RE-KU-RA-I

"A walk"＝アルクコト。

チズ カイテ クレル？
CHI-ZU KA-I-TE KU-RE-RU

"A map"＝チズ。

ショートカット トゥ ベラベラ
SHORT-CUT to BERABERA

get
[get]

the past tense got [gat]
the past participle gotten [gatn]
the present participle getting [getiŋ]

verb =「エル」「トル」
　　　　E-RU　TO-RU

~ヲ テニ イレル ~WO TENI IRERU	**アタラシイ ボールヲ テニ イレル.** ATARASHII BOORUWO TENI IRERU I'll get a new ball.
~ヲ エル ~WO ERU	**イクラカノ スイミンヲ トッタ.** IKURAKANO SUIMINWO TOtTA I got some sleep.
~ヲ トル ~WO TORU	**カレハ スウガクデ エイヲ トッタ.** KAREWA SUUGAKUDE EIWO TOtTA He got an A in math.
~ニ ナル ~NI NARU	**サムク ナッタ.** SAMUKU NAtTA It got cold.
~ヲ ウケトル ~WO UKETORU	**テガミヲ ウケトッタア** TEGAMIWO UKETOtTA Did you get a letter?
~ヲ リカイスル ~WO RIKAISURU	**リカイシマシタ.** RIKAISHIMASHITA I got it.
~ヲ ヨウイスル ~WO YOUISURU	**カノジョハ ユウショクヲ ヨウイシテイマス.** KANOJOWA YUUSHOKUWO YOUISHITEIMASU She is getting dinner.
~(ビョウキ)ニ カカル ~(BYOUKI) NI KAKARU	**カゼ ヒイタ.** KAZE HIITA I got a cold.
~ヲ ツカマエル ~WO TSUKAMAERU	**カレラハ ドロボウヲ ツカマエタ.** KAREWA DOROBOUWO TSUKAMAETA They got the robber.
~ヘ イク ~E IKU	**ドウヤッテ ソコヘ イクノア** DOUYAtTE SOKOE IKUNO How do you get there?

Of course, "get" is a widely used verb and has many meanings in English as well. Remember as many of these phrases as you can.

get BERABERA

get after	オイカケル。 OIKAKERU
get ahead	シュッセスル。 SHUsSESURU
get along	ナカヨクヤル。 NAKAYOKUYARU
get at	テガ トドク。 TEGA TODOKU
get away	タチサル。 TACHISARU
get back	モドル、トリモドス。 MODORU, TORIMODOSU
get by	トオリヌケル。 TOORINUKERU
get down	オリル。 ORIRU
get in	ハイル。 HAIRU
get off	(ノリモノカラ) オリル。 (NORIMONOKARA) ORIRU
get on	(ノリモノニ) ノル。(フクヲ) キル。 (NORIMONONI) NORU, (FUKUWO) KIRU
get out	ソトヘデル。デテイク。 SOTOEDERU DETEIKU
get A out	Aヲ トリダス。 A-WO TORIDASU
get through	トオリヌケル。ツウカスル。 TOORINUKERU, TSUUKASURU
get to	トウチャクスル。ハジメル。 TOUCHAKUSURU, HAJIMERU
get together	アツマル。 ATSUMARU

ショートカットトゥベラベラ
SHORT-CUT to BERABERA

Finally, you have a day off tomorrow!! What do you say?

What time do you get up?

What you say as you're about to leave on your trip abroad:

I've got to check the locks.

What you say when your desk phone rings while you're talking on your cel phone:

Can somebody get it?

What you say to a superior after blowing it the first time around:

Next time I'll get it right!

get

ナンジニ オキル？
NA-N-JI-NI O-KI-RU

"What time"=ナンジ。

トジマリヲ シナキャ！
TO-JI-MA-RI-WO SHI-NA-KYA

"have got to〜"=〜シナキャ。

ダレカ デテクレナイ？
DA-RE-KA DE-TE-KU-RE-NA-I

"Somebody"=ダレカ。

コノツギハ ウマク ヤリマス！
KO-NO-TSU-GI-WA U-MA-KU YA-RI-MA-SU

"Next time"=コノツギ。

ベラベラワンポイントチェック-3
BERABERA one point check-3 [Here are 8 important prepositions]

in

■ ~ノ ナカニ (~NO NAKANI)
カレハ イエノ ナカニ イル. (KAREWA IENO NAKANI IRU)
He is staying in the house.

■ ~ノ トシニ (~NO TOSHINI)
ニセンネンニ ケッコンシタ. (NISENNENNI KEkKONSHITA)
I was married in 2000.

■ ~ノ トキニ (~NO TOKINI)
アメノトキニ デカケタ. (AMENOTOKINI DEKAKETA)
I went out in the rain.

on

■ ~ノ ウエノ (~NO UENO)
テーブルノ ウエノ グラスヲ トッテ. (TEEBURUNO UENO GURASUWO TOtTE)
Pass me the glass on the table.

■ ~ノ ヒニ (~NO HINI)
タンジョウビニ デカケタ. (TANJOUBINI DEKAKETA)
I left on my birthday.

■ ~(カラダノイチブ)ニ (~ [KARADANOICHIBU] NI)
ユビニ ユビワヲ ハメタ. (YUBINI YUBIWAWO HAMETA)
I put the ring on my finger.

at

■ ~(バショ)デ (~ [BASHO] DE)
ツギノ カドデ ミギニ マガッテ. (TSUGINO KADODE MIGINI MAGAtTE)
Turn right at the next corner.

■ ~ニ (~JINI)
ミセハ ゴゼンクジニ アキマス. (MISEWA GOZENKUJINI AKIMASU)
The shop opens at 9am.

■ ~(モクヒョウ)ニ (~ [MOKUHYOU] NI)
カレハ ワタシニ ドナッタ. (KAREWA WATASHINI DONAtTA)
He shouted at me.

of

■ ~ノ (イチブ) (~NO [ICHIBU])
イエノ ヤネハ シロデス. (IENO YANEWA SHIRODESU)
The roof of my house is white.

■ ~ノ ウチノ (~NO UCHINO)
カレラノ ウチノ ダレモ コナカッタ. (KARERANOUCHINO DAREMO KONAKAtTA)
None of them came.

■ ~セイ (~SEI)
ソレハ ナイロンセイ デス. (SOREWA NAIRONSEI DESU)
It's made of nylon.

Prepositions have many meanings depending on the situation in which they're used. We give 3 specific ways of using each preposition. These should be useful in your Japanese study.

to

- **~(ホウコウ)ヘ** (~ [HOUKOU] E)
  カレハ イチルイヘ ボールヲ ナゲタ。 (KAREWA ICHIRUIE BOORUWO NAGETA)
  He threw the ball to first base.
- **~(トウチャクテン)ヘ** (~ [TOUCHAKUTEN] E)
  マイニチ ガッコウヘ アルイテイク。 (MAINICHI GAkKOUE ARUITEIKU)
  I walk to school everyday.
- **~マデ** (~MADE)
  サイゴマデ ハシリツヅケタ。 (SAIGOMADE HASHIRITSUDUKETA)
  I kept running to the end.

for

- **~ノ タメニ** (~NO TAMENI)
  カレノ タメニ カサヲ カッタ。 (KARENO TAMENI KASAWO KAtTA)
  I bought an umbrella for you.
- **~イキノ** (~IKINO)
  オオサカイキノ デンシャニ ノッタ。 (OOSAKAIKINO DENSHANI NOtTA)
  I caught the train for Osaka.
- **~ノ アイダ** (~NO AIDA)
  ソコニ ニシュウカン タイザイシタ。 (SOKONI NISHUUKAN TAIZAISHITA)
  We stayed there for two weeks.

by

- **~ニ ヨッテ** (~NI YOtTE)
  コレハ カレニ ヨッテ コワサレマシタ。 (KOREWA KARENI YOtTE KOWASAREMASHITA)
  This was broken by him.
- **~ノ ソバニ** (~NO SOBANI)
  カレノ イエハ ウミノ ソバニ アリマス。 (KARENO IEWA UMINO SOBANI ARIMASU)
  His house is by the sea.
- **~マデニ** (~MADENI)
  ロクジ マデニ モドリマス。 (ROKUJI MADENI MODORIMASU)
  I'll be back by six.

with

- **~ト イッショニ** (~TO IsSHONI)
  カノジョト イッショニ イキタイ。 (KANOJOTO IsSHONI IKITAI)
  I wanna go with her.
- **~ノ アル** (~NO ARU)
  サンルーフノ アル クルマヲ カッタ。 (SANRUUFUNOARU KURUMAWO KAtTA)
  I bought the car with a sun-roof.
- **~(ドウグ)デ** (~ [DOUGU] DE)
  コノカギデ ドアハ アケラレマス。 (KONOKAGIDE DOAWA AKERAREMASU)
  You can open the door with this key.

ベラベラmoreフレーズ-4
BERABERA more PHRASES -4
Having made such progress recently, what's your next goal?

*Whenever I had an extra 30 minutes in New York,
I'd go for a walk with my camera. Fire fighters, policemen,
and all the people I had just met let me take pictures of them.
The pro wrestler-like policemen were kind of scary though.
The city is awesome!
All the talks I hear are English.
So I felt pretty good when my ears could make stuff out.
If I stuck around, I'm sure my English would improve very quickly.
I want to go again but on my own time.
Definitely! I'm getting more confident, I want to speak more.*

What you say when your date is canceled at the last minute:

How could you?

What you say when invited to a movie:

Who is in that movie?

What you say when asked how you get to work:

I take the train to work.

What you say when someone asks you to do more work but you already have too much:

I'm already too busy.

ソリャ ナイヨ。
SO-RYA NA-I-YO

This is a set phrase.

ダレガ デテルノ?
DA-RE-GA DE-TE-RU-NO

"Who"=ダレ。

デンシャ ツウキン ダヨ!
DE-N-SHA TSU-U-KI-N DA-YO

"A train"=デンシャ。

テンパッテマス!
TE-N-PA-tTE-MA-SU

This phrase is used by young men and women.

What you ask the ticket man on the Shinkansen:

What time will we arrive in Tokyo?

What you say as you're looking over lunch sets A and B:

Which is best?

What you say in the middle of a long conversation:

You know what I mean?

What you say when your test results were just not good enough:

Too bad!

トウキョウニハ ナンジニ ツキマスカ？
TO-U-KYO-U-NI-WA NA-N-JI-NI TSU-KI-MA-SU-KA

"The ticket man"=シャショウサン。

ドッチガ イイカナ？
DO-cCHI-GA I-I-KA-NA

"Which"=ドッチ。

イッテル イミ ワカル？
I-tTE-RU I-MI WA-KA-RU

"Mean"=イミスル。

ダメダァ！
DA-ME-DA-A

"Bad"=ワルイ。

What you say when you're thirsty:

If possible, I'd like something cold.

What you ask when you want to know what's on the daily menu:

What do you have?

What you ask when you want to do a little more sightseeing before your flight:

Would you keep my baggage?

How you respond when invited out to a club:

I'm not in the mood.

ナニカ ツメタイモノハ アリマスカ？
NA-NI-KA TSU-ME-TA-I-MO-NO-WA A-RI-MA-SU-KA

ツメタイモノ="cold drink"。

ナニガ アリマスカ？
NA-NI-GA A-RI-MA-SU-KA

"Have"=アル。

ニモツヲ アズカッテ イタダケマスカ？
NI-MO-TSU-WO A-ZU-KA-tTE I-TA-DA-KE-MA-SU-KA

"Baggage"=ニモツ。

ノリキガ シナイヤ。
NO-RI-KI-GA SHI-NA-I-YA

ノリキ="take an interest"。

What you say when your tooth suddenly starts hurting:

I have a toothache.

What you say when good aromas is wafting from the kitchen:

What's for dinner?

What you say on the phone when the point is not coming across:

Fax me, please.

What you say at the register when you and your friend want to pay for your food:

We'd like to pay separately.

ハガ イタイ!
HA-GA I-TA-I

"A tooth"=ハ。

バンゴハンハ ナニ?
BA-N-GO-HA-N-WA NA-NI

"Dinner"=バンゴハン。

ファクスヲ オクッテ クダサイ。
FA-KU-SU-WO O-KU-tTE KU-DA-SA-I

"~, please."=~ヲ シテクダサイ。

ベツベツニ ハライマス。
BE-TSU-BE-TSU-NI HA-RA-I-MA-SU

"Separately"=ベツベツニ。

What you say at the airport when your bag fails to appear:

I can't find my bag.

What you say to your friend as he runs off to the convenience store:

Buy me some, too.

What you say after just barely making the deadline:

What a relief!

At a club, your answer when asked, "Enjoying yourself?":

This is too much fun.

ボクノ バッグガ ミツカラナイ。
BO-KU-NO BA-gGU-GA MI-TSU-KA-RA-NA-I

"Find"＝ミツカル。

ボクノ ブンモ カッテキテ！
BO-KU-NO BU-N-MO KA-tTE-KI-TE

"Buy"＝カウ。

ホット シタ。
HO-tTO SHI-TA

「ヨカッタ！（YO-KA-tTA）」「アンシン シタ (A-N-SHI-N SHI-TA)」etc.

マジ、ヤバイヨ。
MA-JI YA-BA-I-YO

This phrase is used by boys.「マジ」="really"。

85

What you say after eating something disgusting:

Yuck!

What you say when you wanna spend more time together:

Do you still have time?

What you say at the airport check-in counter:

Can I have an aisle seat, please?

What you say to your friend after dinner:

Have you had enough?

マズイ。
MA-ZU-I

This is spoken more to oneself.

マダ ジカン ダイジョウブ？
MA-DA JI-KA-N DA-I-JO-U-BU

"Still"=マダ。

ツウロガワノ セキヲ オネガイシマス。
TSU-U-RO-GA-WA-NO SE-KI-WO O-NE-GA-I-SHI-MA-SU

"A seat"=セキ。

マンゾク？
MA-N-ZO-KU

「マンプク？ (MA-N-PU-KU)」「オナカイッパイ？ (O-NA-KA I-pPA-I)」etc.

What you say when you want to bargain a little:

How about twenty dollars for three?

What you say when you haven't drunk enough yet:

Let's keep going!

How you answer when someone asks you "What's Tsuyoshi's favorite color?":

How should I know?

How you answer when asked if you're ever played baseball on the North Pole:

I've never done that.

ミッツデ ニジュウドルデハ ドウデスカ?
MI-tTSU-DE NI-JU-U-DO-RU-DE-WA DO-U-DE-SU-KA

"Three (things)"=ミッツ。

モウ イッケン イコウヨ!
MO-U I-kKE-N I-KO-U-YO

This is a common phrase.「モウ イッケン」="one more place"。

ワカルワケ ナイヨ。
WA-KA-RU-WA-KE NA-I-YO

"Know"=ワカル。

シタコトナイヨ。
SHI-TA-KO-TO-NA-I-YO

"Do"=スル。

ベラベラ ワンポイント チェック-4
BERABERA one point check-4 [Homonyms]

As in English, Japanese has many words which have exactly the same pronunciation but entirely different meanings.
Keep your mind flexible and watch out for those Nihon-Go.

	ex.	
アノコト A-NO-KO-TO	that thing	アノコトガ キニナル. ANOKOTOGA KININARU
	with that girl	アノコト ドウイッテルノ? ANOKOTO DOUNAtTERUNO
イクラ I-KU-RA	How much?	コレハ イクラ? KOREWA IKURA
	salmon roe	イクラヲ クダサイ. IKURAWO KUDASAI
イッパイ I-pPA-I	full	オナカ イッパイ. ONAKA IpPAI
	a glass of	モウイッパイ ノム? MOUIpPAI NOMU
オス O-SU	push	ドアヲ オス. DOAWO OSU
	vinegar	オス トッテ. OSU TOtTE
カケル KA-KE-RU	make a bet	カケル? KAKERU
	hang on	コートヲ カケル. KOOTOWO KAKERU
カッテ KA-tTE	Buy!	コレヲ カッテ. KOREWO KAtTE
	selfish	キミハ カッテダナァ. KIMIWA KAtTEDANAA
カンジ KA-N-JI	a feeling	イイカンジ! IIKANJI
	a Chinese character	カンジデ カケル? KANJIDE KAKERU
キタイ KI-TA-I	an expectation	キタイ シテルヨ. KITAI SHITERUYO
	want to come	カレモ キタイラシイ. KAREMO KITAIRASHII
シタ SHI-TA	bottom	シタニ オイテオクヨ. SHITANI OITEOKUYO
	did	ベンキョウ シタ. BENKYOU SHITA
ツイテナイ TSU-I-TE-NA-I	unlucky	キョウハ ツイテナイヨ. KYOUWA TSUITENAIYO
	don't arrive	デンシャハ マダ ツイテナイ. DENSHAWA MADA TSUITENAI
トッテ TO-tTE	pass	オシオ トッテ! OSHIO TOtTE
	a handle	トッテヲ マワシテ. TOtTEWO MAWASHITE
ハラッテ HA-RA-tTE	pay	バッキンヲ ハラッテ. BAkKINWO HARAtTE
	clear away	テーブルノゴミヲ ハラッテ. TEEBURUNOGOMIWO HARAtTE
ヨンデ YO-N-DE	call	キュウキュウシャ ヨンデ! KYUUKYUUSHA YONDE
	read	コノテガミ ヨンデ. KONOTEGAMI YONDE

ショートカット トゥ ベラベラ
SHORT-CUT to BERABERA

have
[hæv]

the past tense had [hæd]
the past participle had [hæd]
the present participle having [hæviŋ]

verb =
「ショユウスル」「モッテイル」「テニ イレル」
SHO-YU-U-SU-RU MO-tTE-I-RU TE-NI-I-RE-RU

~ヲ モツ ~WO MOTSU	アマリ オカネヲ モッテナイ. AMARI OKANEWO MOtTENAI I don't have much money.
~(キョウダイ、コドモ) ガ イル ~GA IRU	カレニハ ムスコガ ヒトリ イル. KARENIWA MUSUKOGA HITORI IRU He has a son.
~(ジカン) ガ アル ~GA ARU	ジカン アル? JIKAN ARU Do you have time?
~(セイカク、シュミ) ガ イイ ~GA II	カノジョハ センスガ イイ. KANOJOWA SENSUGA II She has good sense.
~(シカク) ガ アル ~ (SHIKAKU) GA ARU	クルマノ メンキョガ アリマス. KURUMANO MENKYOGA ARIMASU I have a driver's license.
~(カラダノ トクチョウ) ガ アル ~GA ARU	キミハ イイメヲ シテルネ. KIMIWA IIMEWO SHITERUNE You have good eyes.
~(ビョウキ) デス ~ (BYOUKI) DESU	カゼ ヒイテマス. KAZE HIITEMASU I have a cold.
~(ドウブツ) ヲ カッテイル ~WO KAtTEIRU	ワタシタチハ イヌヲ カッテマス. WATASHITACHIWA INUWO KAtTEMASU We have a dog.
~ヲ ノム ~WO NOMU	コウチャヲ ノミマス. KOUCHAWO NOMIMASU I'll have some tea.
~ヲ タベル ~WO TABERU	オヒル タベタ? OHIRU TABETA Did you have lunch?

ショートカットトゥベラベラ
SHORT-CUT to BERABERA

What you ask the person you just met:

How many brothers do you have?

What you say after dinner:

Let's have dessert!

What you say on the plane:

What magazines do you have?

What you answer when asked when you'd like to have your coffee:

Can I have it later?

have

キョウダイハ ナンニン イマスカ？
KYO-U-DA-I-WA NA-N-NI-N I-MA-SU-KA

"A sibling"=キョウダイ。

デザート タベヨウ。
DE-ZA-A-TO TA-BE-YO-U

"Have"=タベル。

ザッシハ ナニガ アリマスカ？
ZA-sSHI-WA NA-NI-GA A-RI-MA-SU-KA

"A magazine"=ザッシ。

アトデ モラエマスカ？
A-TO-DE MO-RA-E-MA-SU-KA

"Later"=アトデ。

BERABERA one point check-5 [Various adverbs]

ヨク ノミニ イクノ?
YO-KU NO-MI-NI I-KU-NO

How often do you go drinking?

1	**イツモ** I-TSU-MO	always
2	**テイキテキニ** TE-I-KI-TE-KI-NI	regularly
3	**タビタビ** TA-BI-TA-BI	often
4	**トキドキ** TO-KI-DO-KI	sometimes
5	**タマニ** TA-MA-NI	occasionally
6	**マレニ** MA-RE-NI	rarely
7	**メッタニナイ** ME-tTA-NI-NA-I	hardly ever
8	**ゼッタイニナイ** ZE-tTA-I-NI-NA-I	never

When you are asked these questions by someone, please use these adverbs.

	ソレ ホントウ? SO-RE HO-N-TO-U *Is that true?*
1	**ゼッタイニ** ZE-tTA-I-NI *absolutely*
2	**タシカニ** TA-SHI-KA-NI *certainly*
3	**オソラク** O-SO-RA-KU *probably*
4	**タブン** TA-BU-N *likely*
5	**モシカスルト** MO-SHI-KA-SU-RU-TO *maybe*
6	**コトニヨルト** KO-TO-NI-YO-RU-TO *possibly*
7	**ホトンドナイ** HO-TO-N-DO-NA-I *hardly*
8	**ゼッタイナイ** ZE-tTA-I-NA-I *no way*

ベラベラ more フレーズ -5
BERABERA more PHRASES -5

Are you able to study or speak English everyday?

My teacher keeps begging me, "Just 5 minutes of study a day. Please!"
My study materials are always in my bag you know.
It goes without saying!
Each week, he makes a CD talking about the news and
whatever at normal speaking speed.
I listen to it every day over and over.
Lately I think it's helping me to be more aware of English.
The news, movies, soccer broadcasts,
whatever, I turn the TV setting to English.
But Tsuyoshi (Mr. Kusanagi) is studying 8 hours total a day, huh.
I'm not gonna try to compete with that,
but it's my motivation and food for thought.

What you say when someone finds out your little white lie:

I got caught.

What you say when you're about to start a story:

You know what?

What you say when someone requests something a little difficult:

I'll work it out.

What you say to someone who won't stop teasing you:

You are mean.

バレタ。
BA-RE-TA

"A lie"=ウソ。

アノサァ。
A-NO-SA-A

「アノネ (A-NO-NE)」「ネェネェ (NE-E-NE-E)」etc.

ナントカ スルヨ。
NA-N-TO-KA SU-RU-YO

「マカセテ (MA-KA-SE-TE)」「ヤッテ ミルヨ (YA-tTE MI-RU-YO)」etc.

イジワル。
I-JI-WA-RU

"Tease"=カラカウ。

What you say when you can't quite grasp what someone wants to say:

What's your point?

What you say after making a mistake that can't be fixed:

I regret it.

What you ask at the front desk when you have lots of cash:

Can I deposit my valuables here?

What you say when someone's explanation could really use an example:

Like what?

ナニガ イイタイノ?
NA-NI-GA I-I-TA-I-NO

"What"=ナニ。

コウカイ シテルヨ。
KO-U-KA-I SHI-TE-RU-YO

"Regret"=コウカイスル。

キチョウヒンヲ アズカッテ モラエマスカ?
KI-CHO-U-HI-N-WO A-ZU-KA-tTE MO-RA-E-MA-SU-KA

"Valuables"=キチョウヒン。

タトエバ ドンナ カンジ?
TA-TO-E-BA DO-N-NA KA-N-JI

タトエバ="for example"。

What you say when your friend acts like he doesn't know what you're talking about:

Don't give me that.

What you say to a couple after they finish their argument:

You're both wrong.

What you say to your friend who looks a little different today:

That's unusual.

What you say to a friend who won't spare one extra yen for anything:

Don't be so cheap.

トボケルナヨ。
TO-BO-KE-RU-NA-YO

トボケル="pretend"。

ドッチモ ドッチダヨ。
DO-cCHI-MO DO-cCHI DA-YO

This is a set phrase.

メズラシイネ。
ME-ZU-RA-SHI-I-NE

"Unusual"=メズラシイ。

ケチケチ スルナヨ。
KE-CHI-KE-CHI SU-RU-NA-YO

ケチケチスル="be stingy"。

What you say to a friend who looks down about having screwed up:

It's no big deal.

What you say when ordering curry:

Can you make it mild?

What you say after being on the go all day:

Let's call it a day.

What you say after getting the info on a singles party:

I'm looking forward to it.

ソンナ コトモ アルサ。
SO-N-NA KO-TO-MO A-RU-SA

「キニスルナヨ (KI-NI-SU-RU-NA-YO)」「ツギハウマクイクサ (TSU-GI-WA-U-MA-KU-I-KU-SA)」etc.

アマリ カラク シナイデ クダサイ。
A-MA-RI KA-RA-KU SHI-NA-I-DE KU-DA-SA-I

カライ="hot"。

キョウハ モウ オワリニ シヨウ。
KYO-U-WA MO-U O-WA-RI-NI SHI-YO-U

キョウ="today"。

タノシミニ シテルヨ。
TA-NO-SHI-MI-NI SHI-TE-RU-YO

"I'm looking forward to～."=～ヲ タノシミニスル。

What you say when you remember something you had forgotten:

That reminds me!

What you say when your friend won't stop begging you, "Come on, tell me!":

Can you keep a secret?

What you say to your raucously reveling friends:

Don't be silly!

What you say when your computer is on the fritz:

Please, do something!

オモイダシタ！
O-MO-I-DA-SHI-TA

"Remind"=オモイダサセル。

ヒミツニ デキル？
HI-MI-TSU-NI DE-KI-RU

"A secret"=ヒミツ。

フザケルナ！
FU-ZA-KE-RU-NA

「イイカゲンニシロ！(I-I-KA-GE-N-NI-SHI-RO)」「マジメニヤレ！(MA-JI-ME-NI-YA-RE)」etc.

ドウニカ シテヨ！
DO-U-NI-KA SHI-TE-YO

"Do～!"=～シテヨ！

Your answer when asked, "How'd you know?":

Gut feeling.

What you say after not seeing your buddy for a long time:

Would you be Jack?

What you say on the cel phone when someone asks, "Where are you?":

I'm on the way.

What you say to a friend who says, "It's probably OK.":

Did you make sure?

カン ダヨ。
KA-N DA-YO

カン="a sixth sense"。

ヒョットシテ ジャックジャナイ?
HYO-tTO-SHI-TE JA-kKU-JA-NA-I

ヒョットシテ="possibly" or "maybe"。

イマ、ムカッテルヨ。
I-MA MU-KA-tTE-RU-YO

イマ="now"。

チャント カクニン シタ?
CHA-N-TO KA-KU-NI-N SHI-TA

チャント="fully"。

What you say when your explanation doesn't seem to be getting across:

Let me back up.

What you say when your friend's reply seems a bit uncertain:

Don't stand me up.

What you say when your friend's cel phone is ringing:

You have a call.

What you say when your fixing has no effect on the problem:

Nothing seems to work.

イイナオシマス。
I-I-NA-O-SHI-MA-SU

イウ="say"。

スッポカスナヨ。
SU-pPO-KA-SU-NA-YO

"Don't~."=~スルナヨ。

デンワ ダヨ。
DE-N-WA DA-YO

"A cel phone"=ケイタイデンワ。

ドウニモ ナラナイヨ。
DO-U-NI-MO NA-RA-NA-I-YO

「ショウガナイヨ (SHO-U-GA-NA-I-YO)」「シカタナイヨ (SHI-KA-TA-NA-I-YO)」etc.

What you say to your celebrating opponent:

It's not over yet.

What you say when giving directions to the meeting place:

If you get lost, call me.

What you say after dyeing your hair:

It's the thing to do.

What you say when the team you're rooting for loses:

I'm so frustrated.

ショウブハ コレカラ!
SHO-U-BU-WA KO-RE-KA-RA

ショウブ="a match"。

モシ マヨッタラ、デンワ シテ。
MO-SHI MA-YO-tTA-RA DE-N-WA SHI-TE

"Call me."＝デンワ　シテ。

ハヤリ ダカラ。
HA-YA-RI DA-KA-RA

ハヤリ="fashion" or "fad"。

クヤシイ。
KU-YA-SHI-I

「ザンネン (ZA-N-NE-N)」「ガッカリ (GA-kKA-RI)」etc.

BERABERA one point check-6 [Everyday expressions]

セイカツヨウヒン Life articles

chopsticks	オハシ OHASHI
can opener	カンキリ KANKIRI
teakettle	ヤカン YAKAN
pots and pans	ナベ NABE
vacuum	ソウジキ SOUJIKI
laundromat	コインランドリー KOINRANDORII
wall socket	コンセント KONSENTO
intercom	インターホン INTAAHON
scissors	ハサミ HASAMI
book jacket	ブックカバー BUkKUKABAA

タベモノ Food

boiled egg	ユデタマゴ YUDETAMAGO
deep fried chicken	フライドチキン FURAIDOCHIKIN
onion	タマネギ TAMANEGI
cucumber	キュウリ KYUURI
eggplant	ナス NASU
green pepper	ピーマン PIIMAN
custard pudding	プリン PURIN
tea with milk	ミルクティ MIRUKUTII
cream puff	シュークリーム SHUUKURIIMU
soft ice cream	ソフトクリーム SOFUTOKURIIMU

We've all gotten used to Japanese using English words but the truth is we don't really know what a lot of these everyday expressions really mean. So how many do you really know?

ファッション Fashion

jeans	ジーパン JIIPAN
denim jacket	ジージャン JIIJAN
designer label	ブランドファッション BURANDOFAsSHON
custom made	オーダーメイド OODAAMEIDO
tie	ネクタイ NEKUTAI
scarf	マフラー MAFURAA
sweat shirt	トレーナー TOREENAA
conditioner	リンス RINSU
nail polish	マニキュア MANIKYUA
perfume	コウスイ KOUSUI

ショクギョウ Occupations

boss	ジョウシ JOUSHI
company employee	サラリーマン SARARIIMAN
part-timer	アルバイト ARUBAITO
photographer	カメラマン KAMERAMAN
TV star	タレント TARENTO
painter	ガカ GAKA
beautician	ビヨウシ BIYOUSHI
dentist	ハイシャ HAISHA
prime minister	ソウリダイジン SOURIDAIJIN
president	ダイトウリョウ DAITOURYOU

ベラベラmoreフレーズ-6
BERABERA more PHRASES -6
Any comment on the surprising success of BERABERA BOOK?

I'm very happy.
A million people wanted to study English and they chose our book.
It came of my dream of being able to speak English
but apparently a lot of people have the same dream.
It's like a never-ending project for Japanese people.
I really want to be able to speak English.
If you can't speak English,
it means there are a lot of people out there that you can't talk with.
Whenever I meet foreigners at work,
I try to have a conversation with them as long as we have time.
It's just a small cultural exchange
in the grand scheme of things, but I love it!

What you say when the food is a bit bland:

Pass me the salt, please.

What you say when asking your friend to come out:

Will you be late tonight?

Your response to being invited to a class reunion:

I'd love to!

What you say when getting scratcher lottery tickets:

Give me small change, please.

オシオ トッテ。
O-SHI-O TO-tTE

"Salt"=シオ、"sugar"=サトウ。

コンヤ オソイノ？
KO-N-YA O-SO-I-NO

"Late"=オソイ、"early"=ハヤイ。

ゼヒ！
ZE-HI

「ヨロコンデ！（YO-RO-KO-N-DE）」「カナラズ！（KA-NA-RA-ZU）」etc.

コゼニヲ クダサイ。
KO-ZE-NI-WO KU-DA-SA-I

"Small change"=コゼニ。

What you ask your doctor about the medicine he prescribed:

How often should I take it?

What you ask when more work is suddenly thrown on your desk:

When's the deadline?

What you say when your friend is bummed about failing:

Why don't you try again?

What you say at the gas station:

Fill it up, please.

ナンカイ ノムンデスカ?
NA-N-KA-I NO-MU-N-DE-SU-KA

"How often"＝ナンカイ。

イツマデニ シアゲレバ イイ?
I-TSU-MA-DE-NI SHI-A-GE-RE-BA I-I

"A deadline"＝シメキリ。

モウイチド ヤッテミタラ?
MO-U-I-CHI-DO YA-tTE-MI-TA-RA

"Again"＝モウイチド。

マンタンニ シテクダサイ。
MA-N-TA-N-NI SHI-TE-KU-DA-SA-I

"A gas station"＝ガソリンスタンド。

What you say when reminiscing about old times:

I used to play billiards with Mr. Kimura.

What you say when you're looking in the mirror:

I'm tired of this hairstyle.

What you say when you're lost on the subway in New York:

Where should I transfer for Yankee Stadium?

What you say about your friend's nervous leg twitch:

It's habit forming.

キムラクントヨクビリヤードシタモノデスヨ。
KI-MU-RA-KU-N-TO YO-KU BI-RI-YA-A-DO SHI-TA-MO-NO DE-SU-YO

"Used to～" =～シタモノダ。

コノヘアスタイルハアキタヨ。
KO-NO HE-A-SU-TA-I-RU-WA A-KI-TA-YO

"Be tired of～" =～ニ アキル。

ヤンキースタジアムヘハドコデノリカエレバイイデスカ？
YA-N-KI-I-SU-TA-JI-A-MU-E-WA DO-KO-DE NO-RI-KA-E-RE-BA I-I-DE-SU-KA

"Transfer" =ノリカエル。

クセニナルヨ。
KU-SE-NI NA-RU-YO

"A habit" =クセ。

What you say to your friend who's about to start studying Korean:

Jeongmal Book is worth reading.

How you answer to your friend's question, "What do you think our bonus'll be like?":

Don't hold your breath.

What you say when you run into someone in town:

Look who's here! It's Goro!

What you say when the drinks just keep on coming:

That's enough for now.

チョンマルブックハ ヨムカチ アリダヨ。
CHO-N-MA-RU-BU-kKU-WA YO-MU-KA-CHI A-RI-DA-YO

"Worth"=カチ。

アンマリ キタイ スンナヨ。
A-N-MA-RI KI-TA-I SU-N-NA-YO

キタイ="expectations"、キタイスル="expect"。

ダレカト オモッタラ ゴロウチャンジャ ナイカ!
DA-RE-KA-TO O-MO-tTA-RA GO-RO-U-CHA-N-JA NA-I-KA

Sometimes young people call their friends "〜chan".

モウ コレクライデ。
MO-U KO-RE-KU-RA-I-DE

This is a set phrase.

What you say when your friend starts crying over a paper cut:

What's the big deal?

Your answer to the question, "How old are you now?":

I'm pushing 30.

What you say to your friend whose unfinished assignments pour in like Chinese water torture:

You always take your time.

What you say when someone remarks, "You guys are always together!":

I get on well with him.

オオゲサジャナイノ？
O-O-GE-SA-JA-NA-I-NO

オオゲサナ="exaggerated"。

モウジキ サンジュウ ダヨ。
MO-U-JI-KI SA-N-JU-U DA-YO

モウジキ="soon" or "before long"。

マイペース ダネ。
MA-I-PE-E-SU DA-NE

マイペース="one's own pace"。

カレトハ ナカガ イインデス。
KA-RE-TO-WA NA-KA-GA I-I-N-DE-SU

ナカ="a relationship"。

What you say to your loose lipped buddy:

Don't spread it around!

What you say when your friend takes too long to fix something:

There's a little trick to it.

What you say when someone keeps telling you the same thing over and over again:

You're wasting my time.

What you say when your request might just be impossible:

Can something be done?

イイフラサナイデ!
I-I-FU-RA-SA-NA-I-DE

"Spread"＝イイフラス。

コツガ アルンダヨ。
KO-TSU-GA A-RU-N-DA-YO

"A trick"＝コツ。

ジカンノ ムダダヨ。
JI-KA-N-NO MU-DA-DA-YO

"Waste"＝ムダニスル。

ナントカ ナラナイ?
NA-N-TO-KA NA-RA-NA-I

「タノムヨ (TA-NO-MU-YO)」「オネガイ! (O-NE-GA-I)」etc.

What you say when handing over a rough draft:

Just give it a once-over.

What you say when asked to do extra work:

It's such a pain.

What you say at the steakhouse:

Go easy on the garlic.

What you say when you see the prices at a brand name store:

I can't afford it.

ザット ミテ オイテ。
ZA-tTO MI-TE O-I-TE

ザット="roughly" or "about"。

メンドウクサイナァ。
ME-N-DO-U-KU-SA-I-NA-A

メンドウ="troublesome"。

ニンニクハ ヒカエメニ シテ。
NI-N-NI-KU-WA HI-KA-E-ME-NI SHI-TE

"Garlic"=ニンニク。

テガ デナイヨ。
TE-GA DE-NA-I-YO

This is a set phrase in Japan.

What you ask when you want to know who's on the line:

Who's calling, please?

What you say to your friend who comes over for a little fun:

Take your time.

What you answer when asked, "Why don't you tell her how you feel?":

Just because.

How you respond when asked, "Do you believe me?":

By all means.

ドチラサマ？
DO-CHI-RA-SA-MA

"who"＝ドチラ。

ゴユックリネ。
GO-YU-kKU-RI-NE

This phrase is mainly used by women.

ナントナク。
NA-N-TO-NA-KU

In other words, "Without knowing why."

ゼッタイニ。
ZE-tTA-I-NI

Please check p.95, for more explanation.

ベラベラ TRAVEL
BERABERA TRAVEL

イドウ
TRANSPORT

English	Japanese	PAGE
Can I have an aisle seat, please?	ツウロガワノ セキヲ オネガイシマス。 TSUUROGAWANO SEKIWO ONEGAISHIMASU	87
I plan to stay for a week.	イッシュウカンノ ヨテイデス。 ISSHUUKANNO YOTEIDESU	53
Could you put me on the waiting list?	キャンセルマチヲ シタイノデスガ。 KYANSERUMACHIWO SHITAINODESUGA	59
Would you keep my baggage?	ニモツヲ アズカッテ イタダケマスカ？ NIMOTSUWO AZUKATTE ITADAKEMASUKA	81
Let's take a taxi.	タクシーデ イコウ。 TAKUSHIIDE IKOU	9
Is there a taxi stand around here?	コノヘンニ タクシーノリバハ アリマスカ？ KONOHENNI TAKUSHIINORIBAWA ARIMASUKA	17
Keep the change, please.	オツリハ トッドイテ。 OTSURIWA TOITOITE	55
Turn right at the next corner.	ツギノ カドデ ミギニ マガッテ。 TSUGINO KADODE MIGINI MAGATTE	72
Could you turn on the air conditioner?	エアコンヲ イレテ クダサイ。 EAKONWO IRETE KUDASAI	61
Could you let me off here?	ココデ オロシテ モラエマスカ？ KOKODE OROSHITE MORAEMASUKA	61
Where is the nearest subway station?	イチバン チカイ チカテツノ エキハ ドコデスカ？ ICHIBAN CHIKAI CHIKATETSUNO EKIWA DOKODESUKA	53
How much is a round trip ticket?	オウフクキップハ イクラデスカ？ OUFUKUKIpPUWA IKURADESUKA	17
Where should I transfer for Yankee Stadium?	ヤンキースタジアムヘハ ドコデ ノリカエレバ イイデスカ？ YANKIISUTAJIAMUEWA DOKODE NORIKAEREBA IIDESUKA	123
How long until we arrive?	アト ドレクライデ ツキマスカ？ ATO DOREKURAIDE TSUKIMASUKA	19
What time will we arrive in Tokyo?	トウキョウニハ ナンジニ ツキマスカ？ TOUKYOUNIWA NANJINI TSUKIMASUKA	79
I'd like to stay one more night.	モウイチニチ トマリタインデスケド。 MOUICHINICHI TOMARITAINDESUKEDO	17
Fill it up, please.	マンタンニ シテクダサイ。 MANTANNI SHITEKUDASAI	121

Here are some phrases you might find useful as you travel. Learn them (by heart) on the flight over.

カンコウ
SIGHTSEEING

English	Japanese	PAGE
Where is the Japanese Embassy?	ニッポンタイシカンハ ドコデスカ? NIpPONTAISHIKANWA DOKODESUKA	41
How do you get there?	ドウヤッテ ソコヘ イクノ? DOUYAiTE SOKOE IKUNO	68
How long a walk is it from here?	ココカラ アルイテ ドレクライ? KOKOKARA ARUITE DOREKURAI	67
How far is it to Shinjuku?	シンジュクマデ ドレクライ? SHINJUKUMADE DOREKURAI	67
Can we make it?	マダ マニアイマス? MADA MANIAIMASU	47
Will you draw a map?	チズ カイテ クレル? CHIZU KAITE KURERU	67
This road takes you to the station.	コノミチヲ イケバ ツキマス. KONOMICHIWO IKEBA TSUKIMASU	25
Can I deposit my valuables here?	キチョウヒンヲ アズカッテ モラエマスカ? KICHOUHINWO AZUKAiTE MORAEMASUKA	101
How about Shibuya at 6 o'clock?	ロクジニ シブヤデ イイ? ROKUJINI SHIBUYADE II	67
Take a seat, please.	ドウゾ オスワリ クダサイ. DOUZO OSUWARI KUDASAI	22
Hey, I'm in NY!	ニューヨークニ ツイタゾッ! NYUUYOOKUNI TSUITAZO!	15
Can I pick it up?	テニ トッテモ イイデスカ? TENI TOtTEMO IIDESUKA	39
How about twenty dollars for three?	ミッツデ ニジュウドルデハ ドウデスカ? MItTSUDE NIJUUDORUDEWA DOUDESUKA	89
Buy me some, too.	ボクノ ブンモ カッテキテ! BOKUNO BUNMO KAtTEKITE	85
I can't afford it.	テガ デナイヨ. TEGA DENAIYO	131
Can I use yen here?	エンハ ツカエマスカ? ENWA TSUKAEMASUKA	55
What time do you close?	ナンジニ ヘイテンデスカ? NANJINI HEITENDESUKA	19

135

ベラベラ TRAVEL
BERABERA TRAVEL

ショクジ
EATING

English	Japanese	PAGE
Can I make a reservation?	ヨヤクハ デキマスカ？ YOYAKUWA DEKIMASUKA	19
I'll start with a draft beer.	トリアエズ ナマビール. TORIAEZU NAMABIIRU	7
I have a reservation for tonight.	コンヤ ヨヤク シテアリマス. KONYA YOYAKU SHITEARIMASU	65
Can you make it mild?	アマリ カラク シナイデ クダサイ. AMARI KARAKU SHINAIDE KUDASAI	105
Go easy on the garlic.	ニンニクハ ヒカエメニ シテ. NINNIKUWA HIKAEMENI SHITE	131
I'll take some french fries, too.	ポテトモ クダサイ. POTETOMO KUDASAI	43
Can I have it right away?	スグ デキマスカ？ SUGU DEKIMASUKA	17
Let's go somewhere else.	ホカノ ミセニ イコウ. HOKANO MISENI IKOU	33
Pass me the salt, please.	オシオ トッテ. OSHIO TOTTE	119
Looks great!	オイシソウ！ OISHISOU	37
Yuck!	マズイ. MAZUI	87
Have you had enough?	マンゾク？ MANZOKU	87
I'm full.	オナカ イッパイ. ONAKA IPPAI	55
That's enough for now.	モウ コレクライデ. MOU KOREKURAIDE	125
Let's keep going!	モウ イッケン イコウヨ！ MOU IKKEN IKOUYO	89
Can I take this home?	コレヲ モチカエッテモ イイデスカ？ KOREWO MOCHIKAETTEMO IIDESUKA	63
We'd like to pay separately.	ベツベツニ ハライマス. BETSUBETSUNI HARAIMASU	83

トラブル
TROUBLE

English	Japanese	PAGE
My earphones don't work.	イヤホンガ コワレテイマス。 IYAHONGA KOWARETEIMASU	55
I can't find my bag.	ボクノ バッグガ ミツカラナイ BOKUNO BAgGUGA MITSUKARANAI	85
Please, do something!	ドウニカ シテヨ! DOUNIKA SHITEYO	107
Can something be done?	ナントカ ナラナイ? NANTOKA NARANAI	129
Give it back.	ソレ カエシテ。 SORE KAESHITE	11
Stop following me!	ツイテ コナイデ! TSUITE KONAIDE	15
Let's get out of here!	ニゲロ! NIGERO	15
Watch out!	アブナイ! ABUNAI	13
May I leave a message?	デンゴンヲ ノコセマスカ? DENGONWO NOKOSEMASUKA	13
It's an emergency!	キンキュウ デス! KINKYUU DESU	59
I need a doctor.	オイシャサンヲ オネガイシマス。 OISHASANWO ONEGAISHIMASU	41
Call an ambulance!	キュウキュウシャ ヨンデ! KYUUKYUUSHA YONDE	41
I have a toothache.	ハガ イタイ! HAGA ITAI	83
I wasn't thinking.	ウッカリ シテタヨ。 UkKARI SHITETAYO	9
Do you have any cold medicine?	カゼグスリ アリマスカ? KAZEGUSURI ARIMASUKA	39
How often should I take it?	ナンカイ ノムンデスカ? NANKAI NOMUNDESUKA	121
That was close.	キキイッパツ ダッタ。 KIKIIpPATSU DAITA	11

137

カタカナ ハツオン ヒョウ
The list of KATAKANA

ア	A	イ	I	ウ	U	エ	E	オ	O
カ	KA	キ	KI	ク	KU	ケ	KE	コ	KO
サ	SA	シ	SHI	ス	SU	セ	SE	ソ	SO
タ	TA	チ	CHI	ツ	TSU	テ	TE	ト	TO
ナ	NA	ニ	NI	ヌ	NU	ネ	NE	ノ	NO
ハ	HA/WA	ヒ	HI	フ	FU	ヘ	HE/E	ホ	HO
マ	MA	ミ	MI	ム	MU	メ	ME	モ	MO
ヤ	YA			ユ	YU			ヨ	YO
ラ	RA	リ	RI	ル	RU	レ	RE	ロ	RO
ワ	WA			ヲ	WO			ン	N
ガ	GA	ギ	GI	グ	GU	ゲ	GE	ゴ	GO
ザ	ZA	ジ	JI	ズ	ZU	ゼ	ZE	ゾ	ZO
ダ	DA	ヂ	DI	ヅ	DU	デ	DE	ド	DO
バ	BA	ビ	BI	ブ	BU	ベ	BE	ボ	BO
パ	PA	ピ	PI	プ	PU	ペ	PE	ポ	PO

キャ	KYA	キュ	KYU	キョ	KYO
シャ	SHA	シュ	SHU	ショ	SHO
チャ	CHA	チュ	CHU	チョ	CHO
ニャ	NYA	ニュ	NYU	ニョ	NYO
ヒャ	HYA	ヒュ	HYU	ヒョ	HYO
ミャ	MYA	ミュ	MYU	ミョ	MYO
リャ	RYA	リュ	RYU	リョ	RYO
ギャ	GYA	ギュ	GYU	ギョ	GYO
ジャ	JA	ジュ	JU	ジョ	JO
ビャ	BYA	ビュ	BYU	ビョ	BYO
ファ	FA				

Please check these rules for speaking native Japanese.

RULE 1

A small "tsu"= 「ッ」 indicates that the following consonant sound should receive extra stress. It's almost as if there are two of those consonants there. There's no equivalent pronunciation in English but in time, you'll soon hear the difference between 「カタ」="KA-TA (shoulder)" and 「カッタ」="KA-tTA (I won.)"

ッ → a small letter

ex.
オット → O-tTO
キップ → KI-pPU
ウッカリ → U-kKA-RI

RULE 2

A macron = 「ー」, a small "A"= 「ァ」, a small "E"= 「ェ」 and a last "U"= 「ウ」 indicate that the previous vowel sound should be elongated. Here are some examples using English spelling.

アー / アァ → AH
(A+ー) (A+ァ)

ex.
ダメダァ → DA-ME-DA-A → DA-ME-DAH
アノサァ → A-NO-SA-A → A-NO-SAH

イー → EE
(I+ー)

ex.
ビール → BI-I-RU → BEE-RU
タクシー → TA-KU-SHI-I → TA-KU-SHEE

ウー / ユウ → OO
(U+ー)

ex.
キンキュウ → KI-N-KYU-U → KI-N-KYOO
イッシュウカン → I-sSHU-U-KA-N → I-sSHOO-KA-N

エー / エェ → AY
(E+ー) (E+ェ)

ex.
スゲェ → SU-GE-E → SU-GAY
マイペース → MA-I-PE-E-SU → MA-I-PAY-SU

オー / オウ → OH
(O+ー) (O+ウ)

ex.
キョウ → KYO-U → KYOH
チョウシ → CHO-U-SHI → CHOH-SHI

メザセ！トライリンガル!!
MEZASE! TRILINGUAL!!

ベラベラ！
BE-RA-BE-RA

Fluently!

술술.
SUL SUL

ミナサン。
MI-NA-SA-N

Ladies and gentlemen.

여러분.
YEOREOBUN

ナニゴト？
NA-NI-GO-TO

What happened?

뭐야?
MUOYA?

アリエナイ。
A-RI-E-NA-I

It can't be.

있을 수 없어요.
ISSLSU OPSEOYO

イクラ？
I-KU-RA

How much?

얼마예요?
EOLMAEYO?

The trilingual sets of these phrases have same meaning in English, Japanese and Korean.
Learn useful Korean and Japanese phrases together.

カンパイ！
KA-N-PA-I

Cheers!

건배!
GEONBAE!

モウイチド イッテ。
MO-U-I-CHI-DO I-tTE

I beg your pardon.

다시 한번.
DASI HANBEON

オイシイ！
O-I-SHI-I

Delicious!

맛있어요!
MASISSOYO!

ガンバッテ！
GA-N-BA-tTE

Good luck!

파이팅!
PAITING!

マタ アイマショウ。
MA-TA A-I-MA-SHO-U

Let's get together.

또 만나요.
TO MANNAYO

エイゴデウタオウ!
EIGO DE UTAOU!

It Can't Be

Words by Shingo. K
Music by Johan Gunnarsson / Richard Andersson
Arranged by Masaya Suzuki
Chorus arranged by Stephen McKnight

※**1.** Please just wait

Keep believing in me

What did you say?

It can't be, I beg your pardon?

Tell me more about it, you're just joking, no way!

Calm down and everything will be ok!

Is he your type? You've got me

※**2.** Show me your heart

Don't be afraid

What should I do? Tell me

※**3.** If I don't have you

I'm gonna lose my mind

Give me one more chance

So please understand

If I don't have you

My heart would surely die